WORDS OF PROMISE

John Mason
Tim Redmond

PRESENTED TO: *Gary*

BY: *The Clem Clan*

ON: *Happy 40th*

FOR MEN ONLY

WORDS OF PROMISE

Creation House
Strang Communications Company
600 Rinehart Road
Lake Mary, FL 32746
Fax: (407) 333-7100

Send correspondence for authors to:

John Mason and Tim Redmond
P.O. Box 54996
Tulsa, OK 74155

INTRODUCTION

*"Throughout history, long before the Marines,
God has been looking for a few good men," says
Charles Swindoll. Now, more than ever, men around the
world are responding to God—choosing to become men
of integrity, reconciliation and keepers of their word.*

In response to what God is doing, we have created Words
of Promise. *This collection of inspiring quotes brings you
the best of what more than one hundred contemporary
Christian leaders are saying to men today.*

They address these twelve important topics:

- *God*
- *Character*
- *Priorities*
- *Sex and Intimacy*
- *Finances*
- *Family*

- *Dreams and Purpose*
- *Friends*
- *Thought Life*
- *Potential*
- *Ministry*
- *Motivation*

*We believe that when God stretches you,
you never come back to your original shape.
Expect to be challenged, inspired and stretched
as you read this book.*

*Thanks for the privilege of allowing us
to invest in your life.*

JOHN MASON AND TIM REDMOND

PROMISING WORDS ABOUT GOD

FOR MEN ONLY

It is not what we do that matters, but what a sovereign God chooses to do through us. God doesn't want our success; He wants us. He doesn't demand our achievement; He demands our obedience.

CHARLES COLSON

*The counterfeit trinity is me,
myself and I.*

EDWIN LOUIS COLE

*God's forgiveness is not just a casual
statement; it is the complete blotting
out of all the dirt and deep degradation
of our past, present and future.*

BILLY GRAHAM

FOR MEN
ONLY

Every waking moment of our lives, we operate from one of two viewpoints: human or divine. The more popular of the two is human, and the more fruitful of the two is divine.

CHARLES R. SWINDOLL

WORDS OF PROMISE

Who, how and when a man worships determines everything about his life. That is the reason the first promise a man needs to keep is that he'll be honest to God.

JACK HAYFORD

If you are not motivated to spend time with God, then perhaps you have got the wrong idea about the God you are spending time with.

GREG JOHNSON AND MIKE YORKEY

FOR MEN
ONLY

The big picture is simply this:
People turn their backs on God
and God immediately goes to
work to regain fellowship.

CHARLES STANLEY

Four solid facts upon which to build your life: God knows you; God loves you; God cares for you; God has a plan for your life.

RICHARD C. HALVERSON

You are not a human being having spiritual experiences. You are a spiritual being having human experiences.

DENIS WAITLEY

While secular humanists see schools as change agents, there is another change agent, an invisible one, that packs a lot more horsepower. That is prayer.

JAY SEKULOW

---

*A person is healed of burnout
when he receives a fresh revelation
of who God is.*

MALCOLM SMITH

*Prayer is a two-way fellowship in
communication with God. You speak
to God and He speaks to you.
In fact, what God says in prayer is
far more important than what you say.*

HENRY T. BLACKABY

FOR MEN
ONLY

It is an insult to God to allow circum-stances to cause you to fear when the all-powerful Creator of the universe has sworn to stand by you.

CREFLO DOLLAR

When God looks at you, He sees things that everybody else ignores.

MYLES MUNROE

The One who knows you best loves you most!

JOSH MCDOWELL

FOR MEN ONLY

Your renewal will endure, based on the constancy of God's five wonderful words: "I will always love you!"

LLOYD J. OGILVIE

FOR MEN
ONLY

Apart from God, chaos is the norm. With God, the hunger of the mind and heart find their fulfillment.

Ravi Zacharias

If God allowed us to have it the Burger King way—our own way— we would self-destruct.

T. D. Jakes

Don't settle for the world's puny prizes when the Creator of the universe could be your light, your power, your resource, your courage and your purpose for living.

BILL SANDERS

FOR MEN
ONLY

_____

Promising Words About Character

What is staying power?
Remaining. Persevering.
Holding fast. Standing firm.
That's what a man does.
That's what a man is.

Stu Weber

People who stand for nothing will believe in nothing, fight for nothing, fall for anything and eventually fall for something that amounts to nothing.

STEPHEN ARTERBURN

Integrity keeps us from fearing the white light of close examination and from resisting the scrutiny of accountability. Integrity is honesty at all costs.

CHARLES R. SWINDOLL

FOR MEN
ONLY

Nothing is more pathetic than having a small character in a big assignment. Many of us don't want to give attention to our character. We just want the big assignment from God. God develops our character to match our assignment.

HENRY T. BLACKABY

There is a high price for low living.

EDWIN LOUIS COLE

No matter how sound my strategy, how much I study, how hard I work, I'll always be a failure when it comes to being perfect. Yet God loves me anyway. And believing that gives me the greatest sense of peace, calm and security in the world.

TOM LANDRY

A real man is a man of integrity. That means going all out in everything he does. When he says something, you can count on it, take it to the bank.

MIKE SINGLETARY

A man's identity is based on who he is apart from what he does. Identity is a matter of character, not accomplishment; a matter of being and relating, not doing.

STEPHEN ARTERBURN AND DAVID STOOP

A totally secure man lives his private life as if it were public.

LARRY TITUS

---

*Always tell the truth, and you never
have to remember what you said.*

T. L. OSBORN

The trouble with most of us is that we would rather be ruined by praise than saved by criticism.

NORMAN VINCENT PEALE

Integrity demands that there is no hidden agenda, nothing!

RICHARD DORTCH

Loving something that God hates is the ultimate character killer. It literally kills your character from inside.

DEXTER YAGER

*What you are speaks louder
than what you say.*

RON TUCKER

*Nothing and no one can prevent
God's plan from being fulfilled
in your life except your decision
to give up on that plan.*

TOM NEWMAN

FOR MEN
ONLY

When our lives are filled with the husk of prejudice and the chaff of resentment, we have no thirst for righteousness.

BILLY GRAHAM

No test of a man's true character is more conclusive than how he spends his time and his money.

PATRICK MORLEY

———————

A healthy self-image is seeing yourself as God sees you—no more, no less.

JOSH MCDOWELL

PROMISING WORDS ABOUT PRIORITIES

FOR MEN ONLY

The best thing you can do for your kids is to put them on your appointment calendar. Cancel other things to make time with them. No man ever looks back and says, "I wish I'd spent more time in the office and less time with my children."

RANDY ALCORN

Two words in the Christian's language
cannot go together: No, Lord.

HENRY T. BLACKABY

It's time for those who call themselves
men of God to stop wasting time on
frivolous, unimportant programs and
start seriously praying.

WELLINGTON BOONE

The breakfast of Christian champions is early morning prayer.

BILLY JOE DAUGHERTY

*Observe what the unproductive
do and do the opposite.*

JOHN MASON

*Don't let what you cannot do
interfere with what you can do.*

JOHN WOODEN

Some people obviously have the idea that work is a curse, while others look upon it as a calling. Depending upon which view you take, you are spending half of your conscious hours in a generally happy pursuit, or you are largely unfulfilled and unhappy.

D. STUART BRISCOE

*Never complain about
what you permit.*

MIKE MURDOCK

*Proper preparation produces
powerful performance!*

TIM REDMOND

Each morning I ask myself:
What can I take credit for in my life?
The answer is: almost nothing. Even
though I take credit for almost nothing,
I can do all things through Christ.
That's where my power comes from.

JOE GIBBS

Time wasted is destiny deferred.

HAROLD RAY

Unless you predetermine what you need and answer the question, "How much is enough?" you will never reach a position of lasting peace and contentment.

RON BLUE

FOR MEN
ONLY

---

*Most of us do not have unlimited
time to give to our kids. But we
shouldn't allow the enemy to persuade
us that if we don't have a lot of time,
we can't give any time.*

DAVID JEREMIAH

Why should we work ourselves into an early grave, missing those precious moments with loved ones who crave our affection and attention? It is a question that every man must consider.

JAMES DOBSON

People in a hurry never have time for recovery.

ARCHIBALD HART

Somehow, year after year, Dad managed to take us on vacations he couldn't afford to provide, in order to make memories that we couldn't afford to be without. Needless to say, my life is the richer for his commitment.

RICHARD EXLEY

What you measure and monitor improves.

STEPHEN STRANG

Eighty percent of your effort can be saved if twenty percent of your time is first invested in clearly defining the problem.

WILLIAM W. REDMOND

*Goals create priorities,
determine decisions,
dictate companions
and predict choices.*

MYLES MUNROE

WORDS OF PROMISE

PROMISING WORDS ABOUT SEX AND INTIMACY

FOR MEN ONLY

FOR MEN ONLY

A one-woman kind of man has purposefully cultivated a special kind of blindness. In the Old Testament, Job put it this way: "I made a covenant with my eyes not to look lustfully at a girl."

STEVE FARRAR

FOR MEN
ONLY

Men must wake up! Most women are waiting for their men to become as interested and enthusiastic about their marriage as they are about golf, fishing or work.

TONY CAMPOLO

Lovemaking begins in the kitchen with men helping their wives.

JAMES DOBSON

FOR MEN
ONLY

One of the greatest struggles a man experiences in his life is to gather the courage to reach out to his own wife. But if we touch all else and never reach our own, we will die with heavy hearts and empty hands! Stretch out your arms; she is generally closer than she appears!

T. D. JAKES

WORDS OF PROMISE
———————————————

Make your wife's basic needs a priority.

KEN R. CANFIELD

*What would happen if you
suddenly started treating your
wife special all the time?*

GREG JOHNSON AND MIKE YORKEY

*Frankly, sex and marriage
should be a voluptuous experience.
It is a gift to celebrate, excellent
in every way.*

RICHARD FOSTER

I am a role model. Look at me. If I can stay sexually pure, then you can too.

A. C. GREEN

The more a man indulges his sexual appetite outside of marriage, the weaker he becomes. The more he denies his lustful appetite, the stronger he becomes.

LEONARD LESOURD

Love desires to satisfy others,
even at the expense of self.
Lust desires to gratify self,
even at the expense of others.

EDWIN LOUIS COLE

Sex was God's idea, and, with the exception of the idea of salvation, it is the best idea He ever had!

JIM GARLOW

To the extent that we live in sexual purity, we reflect for the whole world that God is at work within us, shaping our desires, choices and actions with more than just hormones.

JERRY KIRK

Many men have asked me, "How do you handle the temptations and offers from women other than your wife?" I always refer them to Hebrews 12:1: "Seeing that we are encompassed about with such a great cloud of witnesses." In addition to not wanting to forfeit my relationship with my own wife and the Lord Himself, how could I commit adultery on a bare stage, with loved ones and angels watching?

PAT BOONE

Once your wife feels understood by you, once she is secure in the non-sexual intimacy of your emotional bonding, she will become more receptive to your sexual overtures.

RICHARD EXLEY

You husbands, be men. Do not be dictators and bosses. Be lovers. Be somebody who will build up, guide, guard and protect your wife.

JOHN OSTEEN

The number one complaint women have in marital counseling sessions is that their husbands don't talk to them. The husband isolates himself emotionally, and communication suffers.

DEXTER YAGER

Promising Words About Finances

Having it all doesn't mean having it all at once. It takes time. Start small and concentrate on today. The slow accumulation of disciplines will one day make a big difference.

JOHN C. MAXWELL

In God's financial order, giving is not just an end in itself. Everything is affected by the spirit of giving.

JACK HAYFORD

There is tremendous freedom of mind in knowing and believing that God owns it all and that money is a resource provided by God to allow us to accomplish His purposes on this earth.

RON BLUE

FOR MEN
ONLY

Borrowing is taking from the future to satisfy the present. Saving is taking from the present to increase the future.

BOB HARRISON

Of the two struggles, I am convinced that prosperity is a much greater test than adversity. Prosperity is far more deceptive.

CHARLES R. SWINDOLL

Put your money to work. View it from a position of what it can do, not just what it can get.

JOHN MASON

Work done for personal gain dulls my spirit; work that produces something beyond myself excites me. Inviting God into my work opens the door for new creativity.

LEONARD LeSOURD

Expect a miracle!

ORAL ROBERTS

The sooner a man becomes satisfied with what he has and stops comparing his financial scorecard and trophies with those of other men, the better he will feel about himself.

STEPHEN ARTERBURN AND DAVID STOOP

FOR MEN
ONLY

The spiritual dangers of borrowing money are two-fold: First of all, borrowing always presumes upon the future, and second, borrowing may deny God an opportunity to work. Getting rid of any debt is a guaranteed profitable investment.

RON BLUE

FOR MEN
ONLY

The secret to financial success is a paradox—money is valuable only when it is saved or shared.

DENIS WAITLEY

Again and again the impossible problem is solved when we see that the problem is only a tough decision waiting to be made.

ROBERT SCHULLER

Men, you need to know that female shopping sprees are not usually the culprit. In 95 percent of our cases, men are responsible because of impulse spending on big-ticket items—cars, boats, airplanes or motor homes—that help create massive debt.

LARRY BURKETT

God did not promise to give us wealth but the power to get it. You will make your way prosperous by learning to think like God and by giving action to your thoughts.

WILLIE GEORGE

The only way to guard against the love of money is to be a giver.

CASEY TREAT

I don't believe for one minute that tithing buys God's blessing. But I do believe that it opens a door—or better, a window—of release for God to bless continually and mightily.

JACK HAYFORD

PROMISING

WORDS

ABOUT

FAMILY

FOR MEN
ONLY

On the day that my daughter was born I was too naive to realize that I was embarking on the most important assignment of my life, and that if I failed as a father, all my other achievements would somehow be diminished.

RICHARD EXLEY

*Never miss the chance to
read your child a story.*

MAX LUCADO

*When was the last time that your
children saw you on your knees
with an open Bible seeking direction
from God? That is an unmistakable
lesson to a child.*

CHARLES STANLEY

How would you finish this sentence? "One thing my dad always said was ..." How will your children finish this sentence?

PAUL LEWIS

Level with your child by being honest. Nobody spots a phony quicker than a child.

JAMES DOBSON

When it comes to transferring our values to our children, much more is caught than taught. The process requires a father's time, a commodity that seems to be in dangerously short supply these days.

TONY EVANS

FOR MEN ONLY

According to the Christian values which govern my life, my most important reason for living is to get the baton--the gospel--safely in the hands of my children. My number one responsibility is to evangelize my own children.

JAMES DOBSON

Being a successful parent requires that you speak two languages—yours and theirs.

DAVID JEREMIAH

When I come home from work and see those little noses pressed against the window pane, then I know I am a success.

PAUL FAULKNER

No *matter how old your children are, it is never too late to unfold your hands and start honoring them.*

GARY SMALLEY AND JOHN TRENT

Your child has many hidden treasures that, once uncovered, polished and held up to the light of encouragement, will lead him to success.

ERIC BUEHRER

The most important hours of the day are when you are home, Dad.

GREG JOHNSON AND MIKE YORKEY

*Invariably, parents make
two common mistakes.
First, they use the same
approach for all their children.
Second, they compare them
with other children.*

CHARLES R. SWINDOLL

Fathering is not a pure science. All fathers fail, but the mark of a true father is what he does after he fails.

KEN R. CANFIELD

The greatest thing a father can do for his children is to love their mother.

JOSH MCDOWELL

*One of my greatest challenges as a
husband and father is to live out in
my home what I proclaim in the pulpit.
In active careers, including the ministry,
you can be out there trying to save the
world yet lose your own home.*

GREG LAURIE

Your son is never too old to hear you say, "I love you; and I'm proud of the man you've become."

JAMES RYLE

Words have an awesome impact. The impressions made by a father's voice can set in motion an entire trend of life.

GORDON MCDONALD

It is a shame we spend more time and energy interviewing people we hire than "interviewing" the people our children associate with.

BOB HARRISON

PROMISING WORDS ABOUT DREAMS AND PURPOSE

FOR MEN ONLY

The only thing that stands between a man and what he wants from life is often merely the will to try it and the faith to believe that it is possible.

RICHARD M. DEVOS

*We must come to a denial of self and a
return to a God-centeredness with our
lives. Then God has us where He can
accomplish through us purposes He
had before He created the world.*

HENRY T. BLACKABY

Seize your destiny.

ORAL ROBERTS

Dealing with success is a real challenge. We must be careful to remember that God brings success. As one man said, "It takes a steady hand to hold a full cup."

GREG LAURIE

Faith is the grit and soul that puts the dare into dreams.

MAX LUCADO

Dreaming illustrates your hidden capacities and your unawakened abilities.

PETER DANIELS

89

---

*Since it doesn't cost a dime to dream,
you'll never shortchange yourself
when you stretch your imagination.*

ROBERT SCHULLER

What you are looking for cannot be found outside of God's will.

STEVE FARRAR

Only change vocations to better fulfill your purpose and maximize your time flexibility, not to make more money.

RUSS CROSSON

Great it is to dream the dream
When you stand in youth
By the starry stream:
But a greater thing
Is to fight life through;
And say at the end--
"The dream is true!"

JOHN OSTEEN

*God never consults your past
to determine your future.*

MIKE MURDOCK

*You've got to have a dream if you
want to make a dream come true.*

DENIS WAITLEY

We become captivated by the height of the mountain rather than our ability to climb when we lose our purpose for making it to the peak.

TIM REDMOND

FOR MEN
ONLY

Life is not worth living without a purpose. Jesus is the purpose that makes life worth living.

Van Gale

With goals, you gain direction; with dreams, you develop momentum; with purpose, you provide increase.

Bob Harrison

You are what God says you are.
You can do what He says you can do.
God has plans for you that are beyond
your wildest dreams. He has planned
for you to live in absolute victory!

BILLY JOE DAUGHERTY

Never make a permanent decision based on a temporary storm. No matter how raging the billows are today, remind yourself: "This too shall pass!"

T. D. JAKES

The greatest tragedy in life is not death, but life without a reason.

MYLES MUNROE

———————

If you are hooked up to your destiny and vision, then the devil cannot affect your tomorrow any more than he can affect your yesterday.

ROD PARSLEY

Promising Words About Friends

FOR MEN ONLY

Until you acknowledge your need for the gifts, talents and perspectives of other men in your life, you will never pursue positive, nurturing relationships.

E. GLENN WAGNER

Don't torture yourself by thinking you have to relate equally to everyone. In fact, don't waste precious friendship time on relationships that won't be productive.

JIM CONWAY

I know you are my friend when you can guard my failures, challenge my thoughts and still celebrate my successes.

T. D. JAKES

_____

All mentors share two things
in common:

1) They believe in you and want
to see you succeed.
2) They are willing to offer themselves
to you to assure your success.

CHIP MACGREGOR

The people with whom you share your goals will play a major part in whether or not you reach the goals.

ZIG ZIGLAR

You are the same today that you are going to be in five years from now except for two things: people with whom you associate and the books you read.

CHARLES "TREMENDOUS" JONES

As I recall, the Bible is very explicit on how I must treat others and strangely silent on how others should treat me.

ROBB THOMPSON

Friendship flourishes at the fountain of forgiveness.

WILLIAM A. WARD

Who holds you accountable? You need someone to whom you can pull out your deepest thoughts and heartaches...we all have blind spots, areas in our lives that hinder our spiritual growth, but areas we cannot see.

REGGIE WHITE

I encourage you to make a list of everyone whom you do not like and begin today to love them by faith. Include those people who have hurt you in the past. Pray for them. Ask for eyes to see them as Christ sees them.

BILL BRIGHT

Few things in this world are more powerful than a positive push. A smile. A word of optimism and hope. A "you can do it" when things are tough.

RICHARD M. DeVOS

We will not have revival until we have reconciliation. We will not have reconciliation until we enter into each other's pain and understand each other racially.

BILL McCARTNEY

Everyone needs a select group of people to whom they can be totally accountable. This group does not have to be large or influential; rather they must simply care enough about you to tell you what you need to hear.

RICHARD DORTCH

*My relationships
determine my results.*

DAVID BLUNT

*The Lord wants to make
us ready for those who
He has made ready.*

LLOYD J. OGILVIE

_Love is an action, not a feeling.
Love is a choice. In fact,
love is a commandment._

MACK TIMBERLAKE

PROMISING WORDS ABOUT YOUR THOUGHT LIFE

FOR MEN ONLY

The mind is the place where decisions are made for or against the truth. What we choose to read, watch and think will determine, to a great degree, whether we will be victims or victors, conquered or conquerors.

GARY J. OLIVER

_____

"Busyness" is one of the enemy's primary weapons. Because of it, we've lost the art and power of quietness, observation and creative thinking.

TIM REDMOND

The atmosphere of expectancy is the breeding ground of miracles.

ROD PARSLEY

Any fact facing us is not as important as our attitude towards it, for that determines our success or failure.

NORMAN VINCENT PEALE

FOR MEN
ONLY

Our thought life is something only we can decide to work on. Most men agree it is a lifelong battle.

GREG JOHNSON AND MIKE YORKEY

A great many of the true saints of God have found their peak spiritual experiences in quietness and solitude.

ARCHIBALD HART

FOR MEN ONLY

Are your problems bigger than life, bigger than God Himself? They aren't. God is infinitely bigger than any problem you do have or will have, and every time you call the problem insolvable, you mock God.

BILL HYBELS

Men without an organized system of thought will always be at the mercy of men who have one.

EDWIN LOUIS COLE

If you want to develop the attitude you'll need to be a hero in business, you can't let yourself think like a victim.

DEXTER YAGER

If you are selective about the things you choose to read, look at or listen to, then you are taking effective action against negative thinking. It's just like with a computer; if you change the input, you will change the output.

ZIG ZIGLAR

God does extraordinary things through ordinary people. Before He does, He changes the way they think.

TIM REDMOND

What you meditate on becomes a part of your life.

DAVID BLUNT

FOR MEN
ONLY

119

One of the most important things for us to learn is how to have the right conversation with the devil...Respond the same way Jesus did: "It is written." Hit him with the Word. Hit him with the Word. Hit him! Hit him! Hit him!

E. V. Hill

If we abide in Him as He abides in us, we begin to see things differently. We begin to look at things with His eyes.

BOB BENSON

When the devil comes knocking at my door, I say: "Lord, would you mind getting that?"

GREG LAURIE

I know of nothing which so stimulates my faith in my heavenly Father as to look back and reflect on His faithfulness to me in every crisis and chilling circumstance of life.

W. PHILLIP KELLER

PROMISING
WORDS
ABOUT
POTENTIAL

God made us, and God is able to empower us to do whatever He calls us to do. Denying that we can accomplish God's work is not humility; it is the worst kind of pride.

WARREN WIERSBE

---

*It doesn't take a big person
to be used of God...but it
takes all there is of him.*

RICHARD C. HALVERSON

*You're born an original;
don't die a copy!*

JOHN MASON

Check the records. There has never been an undisciplined person who was a champion. Regardless of the field of endeavor, you'll find this to be true.

ZIG ZIGLAR

Your perspective of yourself will determine the possibilities that you pursue.

MIKE EVANS

Loving God, loving others and finding value in ourselves—without a doubt, these three aspects of love are the most effective weapons against the destructive power of low self-worth.

GARY SMALLEY AND JOHN TRENT

I've seen common barriers that most often prevent people from performing to the furthest potential. The first is a pattern of past failures and mistakes. The second barrier holding people back is the fear of failure.

TOM LANDRY

FOR MEN ONLY

_____

You are your biggest obstacle to success. Only you can stop God's plan for your life. Others will not stop God.

MARTIN MAWYER

The man who lives for himself is a failure; the man who lives for others has achieved true success.

NORMAN VINCENT PEALE

_You make money doing what
you do best. Concentrate on your
God-given talents and excel in them.
Hire others to do the things you
do not do well._

JAMES E. GUINN

FOR MEN
ONLY

---

*Losers wait for permission to win,
while winners never knew
they needed permission.*

ED MONTGOMERY

*You are very special and unique.
No one on earth has your
fingerprints. Therefore, that
makes you "thumbbody."*

AL BRICE

Grace is the elastic that keeps the child of God from breaking. He learns to stretch until his day of release comes. Then, he is propelled further than he might otherwise have gone.

WILLIE GEORGE

God's not trying to make you into something. He's trying to expose the real you He already sees.

M͏YLES M͏UNROE

Really great men have a curious feeling that the greatness is not in them but through them.

D͏ON R͏USKIN

When people operate in their giftings, they feel a sense of power, grace and fulfillment. That's the way it feels when you serve in an area that uses the gifts God has given you.

TOMMY BARNETT

PROMISING WORDS ABOUT MINISTRY

FOR MEN
ONLY

*The most compelling question
every man must ask is this:
What am I doing today that
will guarantee my impact for
Jesus Christ in the next generation?*

HOWARD HENDRICKS

---

*Win the lost at any cost
because people last forever.*

TED HAGGARD

*The way I know I'm getting
close to God: My heart begins
to echo what His heart is saying—
"Souls, souls, souls!"*

KARL STRADER

When Christians begin to act like Christians and love God, their neighbors, their enemies and especially their Christian brothers regardless of color, race or class, we will see in our time, as in the first century, a great transformation in the whole of society.

BILL BRIGHT

The way I feel about being around unbelievers will tell me a whole lot about my concept of God and how I stand before Him.

JOHN FISCHER

Nothing is more important than leading souls into the eternal kingdom. That is the primary duty of every Christian.

LUIS PALAU

We are being taught now that we must learn the culture of a nation to reach a nation. But you don't reach a nation with culture; you reach a nation with character.

WELLINGTON BOONE

WORDS OF PROMISE

Let me suggest that you go to your pastor and tell him you want to organize a team of men who will pray for him every day.

DALE SCHLAFER

Let my heart be broken with the things that break the heart of God.

BOB PIERCE

FOR MEN
ONLY

If you really believe what the Bible says—that Jesus is the only way, that outside our comfortable church buildings there's a whole world of drifting souls doomed to hell— then you have to be aggressive.

JAY SEKULOW

Your life is the most effective billboard the kingdom of God has.

BILLY JOE DAUGHERTY

God does not call the qualified but qualifies the called!

BILL HAMON

God gets great pleasure from sending His agents on secret reconnaissance missions with personal instructions no one else knows about.

BILL HYBELS

Is your love growing, becoming softer, brighter, more daring and more visible? Or is it becoming more discriminating, more calculating, less vulnerable and less available?

FRANCIS FRANGIPANE

Don't let your wounds interfere with your mission.

STEPHEN ARTERBURN

Oh, if only I could persuade timid souls I meet to listen to that inner voice of the Spirit that challenges us to attempt great things for God and expect great things from God.

TONY CAMPOLO

Promising Words About Motivation

FOR MEN ONLY

Making promises and commitments to change—this is what the Lord requires of us. But, I warn you, this is a powerful, life-changing process.

RANDY PHILLIPS

Good decisions, financial and otherwise, are marked by peace, not panic.

RON BLUE

Let go of whatever makes you stop.

JOHN MASON

FOR MEN ONLY

Luke says Jesus "resolutely set His face to go to Jerusalem" (Luke 9:51, NASB). *He set His face. He locked His eyes on target. He cemented His direction. He was going somewhere. He owned an unshakable purpose.*

STU WEBER

*Impossibilities vanish when
a man and his God
confront a mountain.*

ROBERT SCHULLER

*Adversity causes some
men to break, others
to break records.*

WILLIAM A. WARD

FOR MEN
ONLY

*God does not like the lukewarm,
for He specializes only in the red-hot;
if you have that red-hot burning desire,
then you are going to have results.*

D<small>AVID</small> Y<small>ONGGI</small> C<small>HO</small>

*You can get anything in life
you want if you help enough
other people get what they want.*

ZIG ZIGLAR

*You will never possess what
you are unwilling to pursue.*

MIKE MURDOCK

*Become a "possibilitarian."
No matter how hard things seem
to be or actually are, raise your
sights and see possibilities—always
see them, for they are always there.*

NORMAN VINCENT PEALE

---

*Jesus may call you to walk
on the water but...you'll never know
until you step out of the boat.*

KIM CLEMENT

*In the usual rounds of life, I like to
think of how much God loves me;
when I do that, living with all my
might seems easy to me.*

TONY CAMPOLO

When you and I make a commitment, we must act like a postage stamp: A stamp sticks to one thing until it gets where it's going. It always sticks better if it has taken a licking.

CARLTON PEARSON

_____

*What we taste, touch and tabulate
can never be our satisfaction.*

LLOYD J. OGILVIE

*Take your cue from the mighty eagle.
At the first sign of a storm, he
spreads his wings and climbs above
the tempest. The stronger the wind
the higher he soars.*

NEIL ESKELIN

FOR MEN
ONLY

It's time for men who love Christ to stand up collectively and make their presence felt. If things are going to change, it's got to come through men—through fathers.

BILL McCARTNEY

JOHN MASON
is the author of the best-sellers
*An Enemy Called Average, You're Born an
Original—Don't Die a Copy!* and *Let Go of
Whatever Makes You Stop.* He is a
nationally recognized speaker at
churches and conferences.

TIM REDMOND
is the executive vice president of
the rapidly growing Tax Accounting Software
Corporation and a popular speaker to
leaders nationwide.